London Buses
Around Essex and Hertfordshire

Kevin McCormack

Ian Allan
PUBLISHING

Above: Roofbox RTs were very much in decline by January 1969, when RT3831 was photographed in Rush Green Road, Romford, on route 175. All but one had been withdrawn from public service by 1 July 1970, the survivor holding out until March 1971. *Michael Allen*

Front cover: Route 330 (Hemel Hempstead–Welwyn Garden City Hospital) was officially converted from RT to RMC operation in March 1972 (although RTs continued to substitute for another three years) and became one-man-operated in November 1977, using Leyland Nationals. The end of Routemaster operation of the 330 is thus fast approaching as an immaculate RMC1508 heads along Catherine Street, St Albans, on 21 October 1977. *Michael Allen*

Back cover: The old order still reigns in this view at Loughton station, recorded in May 1969 and depicting RF299 passing RT1359. *Michael Allen*

Previous page: On 3 April 1976 RF428 of Romford garage picks up a fare at Abridge on its way to St Margaret's Hospital, Epping. The bus is displaying new blinds with the route number switched from the offside to the nearside, which was thought to be more helpful to intending passengers. *Michael Allen*

First published 2009

ISBN 978 0 7110 3416 7

Published by Ian Allan Publishing

an imprint of Ian Allan Publishing Ltd, Hersham, Surrey, KT12 4RG.
Printed in England by Ian Allan Printing Ltd, Hersham, Surrey, KT12 4RG.

Code: 0908/B

Visit the Ian Allan Publishing website at www.ianallanpublishing.com

Introduction

London Buses around Essex and Hertfordshire continues the theme originating with *London Buses around Surrey* and *London Buses around Kent*, written by Roy Hobbs and published by Ian Allan in 2004 and 2006 respectively.

This colour album covers the operations of London Transport ('LT') and London Country Bus Services ('LCBS') from 1958 through to 1979, a landmark year which marked the demise in revenue-earning service of the famous RT and RF classes. The photographs in the main body of the book are in date order, consistent with the previous two volumes. With regard to the area covered, Essex and Hertfordshire are defined by traditional boundaries and include those parts which since 1965 have been administered by London Boroughs.

It is worth taking a look at the development of bus and coach services in Essex and Hertfordshire which produced the LT/LCBS operations that are the subject of the photographs in this book. Subsequent changes brought about by the break-up of LCBS and by deregulation and privatisation have had a profound effect on services, operators and vehicle types but are outside the scope of this book. The history of these services is complicated, so what follows is necessarily but a brief summary. The London General Omnibus Company ('LGOC'), which started life in 1855, was the largest bus operator in Central London and from 1912 began running services into the countryside. The East Surrey Traction Co was the main operator in London's country but largely confined itself to Surrey. A significant bus operator in Hertfordshire from 1906 was the London & North Western Railway, which company's services were taken over by the LGOC in 1920, but as a result of differential pay issues (Central Area *vs* Country Area) these were passed on to the National Omnibus & Transport Co, based in Chelmsford. In July 1921 the LGOC signed agreements with East Surrey and National, defining their operational areas and providing buses and garages.

The London Traffic Act of 1924 required all bus routes entering or operating within the Metropolitan Police District to be numbered — the Bassom scheme — which created the basic number series evident in the photographs, the 3xx series, for example, being used for northern 'country' routes.

In the face of competition from independents operating coach services into and out of London the LGOC set up its own Express Department and started its first such service in 1929, the following year creating a new subsidiary, Green Line Coaches. Also in 1929 the LGOC took control of East Surrey, in order to forestall any attempt by the Southern Railway to buy shares in this company. Meanwhile National continued as an operating agent of the LGOC but was split into separate companies, *e.g.* Eastern National, but retained its original identity in the Watford and North London area. To secure its territory in the face of competition from railway companies wishing to operate bus services the LGOC decided to allocate all its country services, including those in the north, to East Surrey, this being reflected by a change of name. Thus it was that in 1932 the East Surrey Traction Co was renamed London General Country Services, and the LGOC's agreement with National was terminated.

Change came again in 1933 with the creation of the London Passenger Transport Board ('LPTB'), whereupon London General Country Services and Green Line Coaches merged to form the LPTB's Country Bus & Coach Department. (For convenience the abbreviation 'LT' is used in this book for operations from this date.)

Nationalisation arrived in 1948 with the creation of the London Transport Executive, replaced in 1963 by the London Transport Board. Then, on 1 January 1970, responsibility for LT's Underground and Central Area bus operations was transferred to the Greater London Council ('GLC'), while the Country Area bus and Green Line coach operations passed to London Country Bus Services, a newly created subsidiary of the National Bus Company ('NBC').

The information contained in this album has been drawn from a variety of sources, but I should like to acknowledge four publications in particular, these being *RT* by Ken Blacker (Capital Transport, 1979), *The Motorbus in London Country* by Kenneth Warren (Ian Allan, 1984), *Glory Days: RF* by Steve Fennell (Ian Allan, 2001) and *London Country in the 1970s* by Steve Fennell (Ian Allan, 2003).

With regard to the supply of photographic material, my heartfelt thanks go to Michael Allen, Maurice Bateman, Michael Wickham, Bruce Jenkins, Chris Evans and Michael Furnell. Pictures taken by Marcus Eavis and Frank Hunt are supplied courtesy of the Online Transport Archive and the Light Rail Transit Association (London Area) respectively.

Kevin R. McCormack
Ashtead, Surrey
June 2009

Left: In terms of public transport the Ilford area will forever be associated with the 43 new South African trolleybuses diverted to London during World War 2 due to the risk of attacks on merchant shipping. These were the capital's first 8ft-wide vehicles and required special dispensation to operate. Originally destined for Johannesburg, 'SA3' No 1763 is seen here at Barkingside. Victims of Stage 3 of the trolleybus-replacement programme, these fascinating vehicles would run in service for the last time on 18 August 1959. *Frank Hunt / LRTA*

Above: The 84-strong Guy Special (GS) class, designed for one-man operation (OMO), was introduced in 1953 to replace Leyland Cubs (C class) on less-busy, rural routes. However, as early as 1958, when this photograph of GS83 was taken at Bovingdon, GS disposals had commenced due to OMO conversion of RFs, which were able to displace them. The 316 service (Chesham–Hemel Hempstead) had its origins in Amersham & District route 16 and was acquired by the LPTB in 1933. *Michael Wickham collection*

A 'K2'-class Leyland trolleybus dating from 1939, No 1345, passes the Eleanor Cross at Waltham Cross in 1961. The vehicle is heading for Liverpool Street station on route 649, which would succumb to Stage 11 of the trolleybus-replacement programme, running for the last time on 18 July 1961. *Marcus Eavis / Online Transport Archive*

RT3613 prepares to swing into Romford garage at the end of its journey from Tilbury Ferry in June 1965. Route 370's origins go back to National's service 40 from Grays to Upminster, which started in October 1924 and became a joint operation with the LGOC when extended to Romford in December 1928. The route passed to the LPTB in 1933 and was renumbered the following year, the extension to Tilbury Ferry being introduced in January 1952. *Maurice Bateman*

Left: Route 800 was not, of course, a Central Area service, but in the winter of 1965/6 some red RTs, including RT1330, covered a temporary shortage of Country Area examples at Stevenage. At least the loan would have helped to wean the local population off green-liveried buses and acclimatise them to the variety of colours that would follow in a few years time on Stevenage town services!
Maurice Bateman

Above: With cream central relief band and upper-case lettering on the 'via' blind (lower-case lettering having been introduced from 1961) RT2981 looks rather dated in this photograph taken on 21 August 1966 in Exchange Road, Watford. Route 158 was cut back from Watford to Harrow Weald on 13 June 1970 and withdrawn completely on 30 October 1971, as OMO gradually permeated the Harrow area.
Maurice Bateman

Above: Two Guy Specials at Rickmansworth, and neither of them working the 336A service, with which the type is particularly associated! In this view dating from May 1967 GS57 is passing through on route 309 (Harefield–Chorleywood) while GS15 lays over on a short-working of the 309A (Northwood–Chorleywood). RFs were shortly to take over these routes, the 309A being withdrawn in 1972. *Michael Wickham collection*

Right: Introduced in 1962 and based on prototype 'coach' Routemaster CRL4, the 68 RMCs, together with the 43 longer RCLs, were intended to provide a more luxurious ride on busy, long-distance Green Line services. However, their heyday turned out to be brief, as passenger numbers declined through increased car ownership, and OMO was necessarily introduced. Route 708 was so converted in February 1969, exactly one year after this picture was taken of RMC1505 at Hemel Hempstead, northern terminus of the 708. *Michael Wickham collection*

Left: A total of 85 RTs wore Green Line livery, with no advertisements, but in the late 1960s these were relegated to bus work and lost their unique appearance. Nevertheless, green RTs (not necessarily ex-Green Line examples) continued to be used on Green Line relief duty, as demonstrated at Harlow garage by RT3895, standing alongside RF648 in April 1968. Harlow garage opened in 1963, replacing Epping garage. *Michael Wickham collection*

Right: In order to present a more contemporary image of Green Line coach services following the introduction of the modern-looking RC class 175 RFs, by then around 15 years old, were refurbished between 1965 and 1967 as part of an attempt to disguise their age. This view of Marlowes, Hemel Hempstead, in April 1968, features modernised RF80, operating on route 719 from Wrotham, Kent, via Victoria, while passengers board RT630 for a trip to Bennett's Gate on local service 314A. *Michael Wickham collection*

Left: An example of a fast-disappearing species, roofbox RT2184 makes its way through Hornchurch in January 1969. Route 66 (nothing to do with the American TV series!) was converted from RT to SMS operation on 8 January 1972. *Michael Allen*

Above: Nine experimental Strachans-bodied 'Merlins' (in reality AEC Swifts) were allocated to the Country Area, but following Union opposition to their introduction XMB15 became the only one to enter service. That was in early 1969, when this picture at Tring garage was taken, by which time the bus was three years old and had been twice re-registered. In the background stand Tring's two Aldenham staff buses — roofbox RT329 (one of the last four RT3-bodied examples still in stock) and RT1866. *Bruce Jenkins*

Left: Green Line-liveried RT999 passes Tring garage in the spring of 1969, by which time it had been demoted to bus work. However, RTs continued on Green Line relief workings into the 1970s, while from June 1976 to February 1977 (two months before its closure) Tring garage employed an RT not merely as a relief vehicle but in regular peak-hour service on Green Line route 706! *Michael Allen*

Above: These RTs pictured on route 150 at Chigwell Row on 26 April 1969 are wearing slightly different liveries. RT2240 in the foreground must be due for overhaul, because it still has a cream central relief band despite the change from 1965 to grey, as seen (albeit here looking more like white) on the bus behind. *Michael Allen*

Left: In 1969 route 150 terminated outside the Beehive public house at Lambourne End, where RT2568 is seen on 26 April. Despite being replaced at weekends by RMs from 28 February 1976, RTs remained on weekday services until DMS-class Fleetlines took over on 15 October 1977, from which date the route was also cut back from Lambourne End to Chigwell Row. *Michael Allen*

Above: In the deceptively rural setting of Hemnall Street, behind the High Street, RF511 rests at the Epping Town terminus of route 250 in May 1969. This vehicle would be one of three (the others being RF510 and RF512) accorded the honour of being the last Central Area RFs to carry fare-paying passengers, being used on a farewell tour from Kingston on 31 March 1979, the day after the type ceased to operate scheduled services. *Michael Allen*

Left and above: St Albans garage, opened in 1936, was typical of the substantial brick-built bus garages constructed prewar by LT for the Country Area. Closed in January 1989, it was eventually demolished following the failure of a preservation scheme. In the first of two views dating from May 1969 Green Line-liveried RT650 is parked in the front of the garage alongside Country Area bus RF662, while in the second modernised Green Line coach RF142 and former coach RF231 stand at one of the entrances. *Michael Allen (both)*

Above and right: Central Area route 84 was unusual in venturing far into Country Area territory, running as far north as St Albans. This service began in 1912 and used to run to Golders Green but was later cut back to Arnos Grove and then curtailed to New Barnet when Merlins replaced RTs on 23 August 1969. The route was operated from Potters Bar garage, a Central Area garage itself somewhat remote from the capital, and from Palmers Green on Sundays. These photographs taken in May 1969, just three months before the RTs were ousted, feature RT2043 standing on the forecourt of St Albans garage and also passing the White Hart at South Mimms.
Michael Allen (both)

Above: Loughton-based RF316 stands in the grounds of St Margaret's Hospital, Epping, in May 1969 on short-lived route 20B. Introduced on 3 October 1965 to replace crew (RT) operation on the northern section of route 20, the 20B had the distinction of being the first single-deck route since 1934 to be numbered below 200 but was withdrawn on 14 June 1969, when it once again became part of route 20, upon the latter's conversion from RT to OMO Merlin operation. *Michael Allen*

Right: Another photograph from May 1969 taken in Epping, but this time in the High Street and depicting a Country Area Routemaster bus, RML2444, working a Green Line relief service. As part of the elimination of cross-London running of these services the 718 (Windsor–Harlow) was curtailed from 2 April 1977 to operate between Windsor and Victoria. *Michael Allen*

It's still May 1969 in Epping, and now the focus is on Station Road, where RT797 is seen on route 339. Running from Harlow to Warley, this marked the eastern boundary of LT's operations in Essex and, as the N9, had passed from National to London General Country Services in 1932, being renumbered two years later. *Michael Allen*

A variant of route 341 (St Albans–Hatfield–Hertford) was the shorter 341B, which served Hatfield South via Woods Avenue. In May 1969 RT935, one of several Central and Country RTs outshopped in 1966 with experimental cream fleetnames instead of the more sober (and, thankfully, retained) gold-coloured version, passes St Peter's Church in Catherine Street, St Albans. *Michael Allen*

Above and right: Lowbridge AEC Regent IIIs (RLH class) were few and far between in Essex and Hertfordshire. Green examples would venture from Chesham to Watford on route 336, while in Essex a low bridge in St Mary's Lane, Cranham, necessitated the retention of four red ones at Hornchurch garage to operate route 248 to Upminster until Swifts took over in September 1970. The 248A was a Mon-Fri peak-hour variation running only between Upminster and Corbets Tey

and requiring just one vehicle, this being an RLH (there being one spare), although there were no low bridges along this section; with a 6-minute journey time, it was also London's shortest bus route. In these views from June 1969 RLH65 stands at the Upminster (Hall Lane) terminus of the 248, while RLH52 heads along Corbets Tey Road, Upminster, on the 248A. Both buses would subsequently be exported to North America. *Michael Allen (both)*

The 248A service (see previous page) met up with route 370 (Tilbury Ferry–Romford) at the Huntsman & Hounds public house at Corbets Tey, where, also in June 1969, RT3624 is pictured.

Ex-Green Line RMCs, demoted following the introduction of the RP coaches, replaced RTs on route 370 during 1972. *Michael Allen*

In August 1969, less than six months before the takeover by LCBS of LT's Country Area services, a trio of immaculate RTs congregate at Stevenage bus station, with RT963 in the foreground. By the end of the year a radical shake-up of this expanding New Town's local services would begin, and sights such as this would quickly pass into history. *Michael Wickham collection*

Left and below left: In the days before compulsory crash helmets a motor scooter overtakes RT1539 in Cranbrook Road, Ilford on 19 April 1970 while, almost simultaneously, RT446 approaches from the opposite direction. July 1971 would see the end of RTs on both these services, the 167 being converted to SMS operation and the 150A withdrawn. *Michael Allen (both)*

Right: Further east, RT3877, still displaying LT roundels despite its change of ownership, occupies the pull-in alongside Grays bus garage, working route 328 (Bulphan–Aveley) on 1 June 1970. The RMC behind also maintains a strong LT appearance. *Michael Allen*

Left, below left and right: Judging by these three photographs, taken on 1 June 1970, LCBS was having a bad day with blinds in the Grays area! RT3241 is undoubtedly going to South Ockendon (presumably the station) and is seen in South Road, South Ockendon, still wearing its LT radiator badge. Meanwhile RT4507, pictured in Grays, is actually working route 368 rather than the 374. Finally RT860 emphasises its operation of route 369 as it manœuvres at Ockendon station.
Michael Allen (all)

With very little room to pass another vehicle here in Loudwater Lane on 5 June 1970, GS33 clearly demonstrates why only this type was suitable for route 336A (Rickmansworth–Loudwater Estate). The retirement of the regular driver, who lived on the estate (where the bus was kept overnight in an old coach house instead of being returned to Garston garage), was a factor in the decision to withdraw this, the last GS-operated service, on 30 March 1972.
Michael Allen

The 287, from Barking to Brentwood (Hornchurch Garage–Brentwood from 31 December 1966), was a relatively short-lived service, being introduced in 1962 and withdrawn on 18 July 1970 when routes in the Romford area were reorganised. With less than a month to go, RT875 pauses in Main Road, Gidea Park, on 20 June 1970. *Michael Allen*

Above and right: RT operation of route 174 officially ceased in July 1966, when Routemasters took over, but RTs were subsequently reinstated for some Saturday journeys, this situation continuing until March 1977. On 20 June 1970 RT2954 stands at the route's rural Noak Hill (Pentowan) terminus, where it would have to undertake a tricky three-point turn before heading back to Dagenham. The crew are clearly pleased to have an RT! *Michael Allen*

Left: Of the 76 members of the RLH class around two-thirds were new as Country Area vehicles, so it is perhaps ironic that the last RLH routes (178, 248 and 248A) should have been in the Central Area, although those on the 248 group outlived their last Country cousins by little more than six weeks. On 13 July 1970 RLH71 stands at the Cranham terminus of the 248, at the junction of Front Lane and Moor Lane and opposite the entrance to Upminster Underground depot. *Michael Allen*

Above: The RF fleet originally totalled 700 vehicles, of which LCBS inherited 413 on 1 January 1970. Although by then almost 20 years old they found favour with their new owner on account of their having been converted to OMO. On 1 August 1970 RF664 stands resplendent outside St Albans City station on route 342 (London Colney–Dunstable). *Michael Allen*

Left and below left: These scenes in central Harlow on 29 August 1970 illustrate how little vehicles changed in appearance in early LCBS days. The removal of the LT bullseye motif between the headlights is the only indication of a change of ownership for 'modernised' RF155, which remains in Green Line livery and still carries the traditional roof boards for its journey from Bishop's Stortford to Aldgate. Meanwhile RML2442, working local town service 805, remains unaltered but for the loss of its LT radiator badge and the acquisition of a gold London Country fleetname. *Michael Allen (both)*

Right: In the depths of winter RT4768 and RF225 look less than pristine as they stand in St Mary's Square, Hitchin, on 23 January 1971. Route 303A, introduced in 1937, was a variation of the original National route N7 (later 303), diverting to serve Brookmans Park station and Welham Green. The 386 was an infrequent rural service which on Tuesdays, Thursdays and (as here) Saturdays linked Hitchin with Hertford by way of Stevenage and Buntingford. *Michael Allen*

Left and above: On a sunny 13 February 1971 two very different LCBS vehicles pass through Hatfield on Green Line service. RT4514, not one of the 85 RTs previously painted in Green Line livery, masquerades as a coach as it heads along Queensway on the 716A from Woking to Stevenage, while in St Albans Road a very smart coach, RF95, modernised and by now adorned with the short-lived 'flying Polo' motif, works a 724 'Express' journey from Romford to High Wycombe. *Michael Allen (both)*

Left: RT3232 pauses in Marlowes, Hemel Hempstead on 22 February 1971. Note that despite more than 13 months of LCBS ownership it has managed to retain its LT radiator badge, which would have come in useful (were it not of the wrong colour) in September 1972 when this bus, along with 33 other redundant RTs, was purchased by LT as a short-term expedient to cover a chronic shortage of serviceable vehicles. Behind is Merlin MBS298, the ubiquity of this type, along with the later SM class, being the main reason for the RT surplus, as well as the cause of subsequent reliability problems! *Michael Allen*

Below: Interest in the photographer's activities is charmingly expressed on the top deck of RT4640 as the vehicle stands at Wanstead station on 27 February 1971 in the company of RML2513. Apart from some Saturday workings (which continued until 16 June 1973) route 101 was converted to Routemaster operation on 28 October 1972. *Michael Allen*

Left: With only two weeks to go before Swifts took over the 252 service, Romford garage's RT3024 proceeds along Coronation Drive, Elm Park, on 27 February 1971. Historically, numbers in the 2xx series were allocated to routes operated by single-deckers, but RTs had replaced the Leyland Tigers (TD class) on the 252 in 1958. The new era of single-deck operation was destined to be short-lived, the Swifts being superseded by DMSs in 1975. *Michael Allen*

Above: RM, RT and RF classes are all represented at Chingford station in this view dating from May 1971. RF390 is operating route 121, which became OMO on weekdays when RFs replaced RTs on 7 August 1966, although conversion of Saturday services was not effected until 14 June 1969. Route 69, here in the hands of RM136, was introduced on 3 February 1960 as a bus replacement for trolleybus route 669 and was subsequently extended to Chingford. *Michael Allen*

Left and above: Stevenage town services underwent various transformations with eye-catching liveries. The first of these made its appearance on 29 December 1969 (three days before the LCBS takeover), a striking blue and silver having been applied to three Daimler Fleetlines dedicated to two 'Blue Arrow' routes; marketed as personal taxi services, stopping anywhere convenient and with reserved seats for passengers (all season-ticket-holders), these lasted until April 1972. On 31 July 1971 the first Superbus service was launched, using five Swifts (SMs) and two Metro-Scanias (MSs) painted yellow and blue. These photographs, taken in August 1971, depict XF6 and MS1, the traditional image being represented by RT3247. *Bruce Jenkins (both)*

A 1970s fad, to which LCBS succumbed to a limited extent, was to cover buses in all-over advertising. On 26 March 1973 former Green Line coach RMC1516 departs St Albans' Marshalswick Estate for Hertford on route 341, which did not serve the store being promoted. *Maurice Bateman*

On 7 May 1973 RT994 leaves the Apsley Mills industrial estate on a works journey. The bus looks as smart in its LCBS livery as it would have looked in LT days, albeit more colourful, but would not have found favour with the National Bus Company, which the previous year had imposed its corporate image on all subsidiaries — a policy which LCBS, fortunately, was slow to implement. *Maurice Bateman*

Above: The 383 was a local Hitchin route serving the Oakfield and Purwell Lane housing estates and was operated by RFs from Stevenage garage until AEC Reliance (RP) coaches took over in May 1976. RF165 is pictured on 8 May 1973. *Maurice Bateman*

Right: Red and green meet in Woodford Road, Watford, as a Harrow Weald Merlin, MB168, passes a smart-looking LCBS double-decker, Garston's RML2435. The date is 2 July 1973. *Maurice Bateman*

A vehicle which should need little introduction: the fourth and final Routemaster prototype. This Green Line Routemaster with unique Eastern Coach Works bodywork entered service as CRL4 (**C**oach **R**outemaster **L**eyland) on 9 October 1957. Latterly just plain RMC4, working from Hertford garage, it is seen on 17 May 1974 waiting to depart Welwyn Garden City station on local works service 845 to Great Ganett. *Maurice Bateman*

STH OXLEY and KINGSWOOD

346 Hallows Crescent
Heysham Drive

PAY AS YOU ENTER
PLEASE

LONDON TRANSPORT

VLW 479G

Once the loan of some Central Area RFs to the Country Area, which spanned the transfer to LCBS, had come to an end, no one expected that LT red buses would ever again cover for green examples. However, in 1974 LCBS was facing such a dire vehicle shortage, due mainly to the unreliability of newer buses, that it was reduced to hiring buses from other operators, and, in desperation, this included several surplus Merlins from LT, among them MBS479, pictured at South Oxley on 14 October 1974 working Watford local service 346. *Maurice Bateman*

Above: Garston garage was particularly badly affected by unserviceable vehicles, in this case mainly by Routemasters overdue for overhaul. Route 306 (New Barnet–Leavesden) was officially crew-operated with RMLs until September 1976, but in this view at Bushey Heath on 5 February 1975 ex-Green Line RF85 is substituting.
Maurice Bateman

Right: Aldenham Works, located at Elstree, was built as an Underground depot for the Northern Line following the proposed extension to Bushey Heath (subsequently abandoned) and in 1955 was converted into a bus-overhaul works. It specialised in body and chassis overhaul, enabling Chiswick Works to concentrate on overhauling running units. Workers were transported in from local garages by a fleet of staff buses, which at the time of this photograph, taken on 10 April 1975, consisted entirely of RTs; nearest the camera are RTs 4614, 2224 and 2411. Aldenham Works was to close in November 1986, the building being demolished 10 years later.
Michael Furnell

Left: From 1973 to 1976 Potters Bar, which was 'moved' from Middlesex to Hertfordshire in 1965, had a famous local resident in the shape of the unique rear-engined, front-entrance OMO Routemaster, FRM1. Intended to be the forerunner of a new class (which never materialised) it first entered service in 1966 and would end its career on the Round London Sightseeing Tour, finally being withdrawn in 1983 and passing into preservation. In this view dating from 1 April 1975 FRM1 socialises with an RF replacement, BN41. *Chris Evans*

Above: Both RMC1504 and SNC95 were built as Green Line coaches but had been relegated to bus work by the time of this view at Two Waters (Hemel Hempstead) garage on 12 May 1975. The RMCs spent 10 years on Green Line duties, from 1962 to 1972, whereas the early short Leyland National 'coaches' were demoted much sooner, on account of their unsuitable interiors. *Michael Allen*

Left: Following overhaul at Aldenham in 1972 RT3752 had the distinction of being painted in a shade lighter than traditional Lincoln green but darker than NBC leaf green, the latter first being applied to an RT in December 1974. The vehicle is depicted near Two Waters garage on 12 May 1975, its three-year-old paintwork lasting well. *Michael Allen*

Above: LT shared LCBS's problem of having insufficient serviceable buses and in 1975 purchased from British Airways 13 forward-entrance Routemasters, as a precursor to buying the airline's entire fleet of 65 vehicles. LT put this initial batch on Romford garage's route 175, on which they lasted just under a year. There being no provision for a blind display, the route details were carried on a slip-board beneath the front canopy. RMA11, seen passing Daimler Fleetline DMS742 in St Edward's Way, Romford, on 21 February 1976, still wears BEA dark-orange livery. *Michael Allen*

RF690, the last survivor of this class at Grays, has just passed St James's Church at West Tilbury on its way from Linford on 25 March 1976. Route 374 was subsequently converted to BN operation, RF690 being transferred to Dartford to finish its days there. The church would be declared redundant in November 1980. *Michael Furnell*

There's something wrong here at the Mill Road terminus at East Purfleet, and not just the baby in the arms of faceless parents! Route 300 (Purfleet–Stifford Clays), which decorated RMC1490 is purporting to work, was renumbered 375 in February 1974 to allow the number 300 to be used for the former 303A service (Hitchin– New Barnet); the trouble is that this photograph was taken more than two years later, on 25 March 1976, and the route number has not yet been amended! *Michael Furnell*

Above: The now closed Bata shoe factory was a major employer in the Purfleet area, with its own residential estate for workers. Over the years it was served by various bus routes, and in this view dating from 31 March 1976 RMC1501 of Grays garage has arrived at the factory on a 374 journey. *Michael Allen*

Right: A red RT route which brought these vehicles into the countryside was the 247, on which North Street (Romford)-based RT4205 is seen operating at Great Warley shortly before Bristol LHs single-deckers (BLs) took over on 24 April 1976. *Michael Allen*

Above: Passengers pile onto RF428 at Havering-atte-Bower on 3 April 1976, no doubt unaware that BLs will be taking over later in the month; indeed, route 250 would be withdrawn on 8 January 1977, being subsumed within the 247. However, RF428 lived on, being recertified to help meet a continuing requirement for RFs at Kingston, which was to last until 30 March 1979. *Michael Allen*

Right: Another rural outpost for red RTs was Abridge, where RT1929 is seen on 3 April 1976 at the terminus outside the Blue Boar inn. This single-bus operation from Loughton was introduced on 7 September 1968 and withdrawn a week after this photograph was taken, as a result of the GLC's curtailment of subsidies for services beyond its boundaries. *Michael Allen*

Above: Wearing a striking livery of pale grey with green waistband, 14 AEC Reliance coaches (RCs) entered Green Line service in 1965. Unfortunately the high standard of comfort and vision (through the enormous windows) was not matched by mechanical reliability, and in April 1974 the 13 survivors (one having been destroyed by fire) were relegated to bus work at Hertford garage, where they remained until withdrawn from public service in January 1977. RC7, adorned with all-over advertising, proceeds through Ware on 7 March 1976.
Michael Allen

Right: No modern-day cycling garb for the girl in pink watching RMC1474 as it passes Ware War Memorial on 7 May 1976. In line with LCBS policy of dispensing with suffix route numbers the 331A service became the 337 in May 1974, but, again, there has been a significant delay in the fitting of new blinds, two years having elapsed already.
Michael Allen

The vehicle shortages being experienced by LT in the mid-1970s resulted in the hiring in September 1975 of 10 Leyland Titan PD3s from Southend Corporation. When no longer required they were passed on to LCBS, entering service at Harlow from 29 March 1976. Replacing RTs, they stayed until January 1977. Southend No 336 is depicted entering Bishops Stortford on 31 August 1976. *Michael Allen*

RT-operated route 175A was withdrawn on 8 January 1977 and replaced by new route 247B (Romford Station–Ongar) worked by recently delivered Bristol LHs (BL class). In this busy scene, recorded on 1 July 1977, passengers are boarding BL11 in South Street, Romford, close to the railway station. On 5 January 1980 BLs would be replaced on this route by Leyland Nationals. *Michael Allen*

Above: In 1971 LCBS purchased 15 AEC Swifts from South Wales Transport, designating them SMW. Twelve were Willowbrook-bodied vehicles which were based at St Albans, where SMW9, in the company of Merlin MBS437, is pictured in St Peter's Street on 16 July 1977. The SMWs lost their attractive chromium embellishments, or had them painted over, upon overhaul. *Chris Evans*

Right: LCBS's first new double-deckers were 11 Daimler Fleetlines (the AF class) which entered service in February 1972, to be followed two months later by the first of the AN class of Leyland Atlanteans, of which initial deliveries comprised 120 vehicles. The first 90 were bodied by Park Royal, among them AN41, photographed on 22 October 1977 in the special livery celebrating HM The Queen's Silver Jubilee. The busy street scene is St Albans Road, North Watford. *Chris Evans*

Above: The 90-strong RP class (**R**eliance/**P**ark Royal) were OMO coaches introduced by LCBS to replace crew-operated RMCs and RCLs on Green Line services. However, they were not particularly reliable and were gradually demoted to bus work, replaced on Green Line services by a new generation of coaches. Nevertheless, some remained in stock for as long as 12 years — not a bad record for early-1970s vehicles. RP2 entered service in December 1971 and is seen here working route 343 (Dunstable–Hatfield) at Welham Green on 21 October 1977. *Michael Allen*

Right: The penultimate RT-operated service was Barking's route 87, which was converted to RM operation (except for one Saturday working) on 28 October 1978. Having just left the Abbey Wood Lane terminus at Rainham, RT2671 passes a man opening an umbrella in Upminster Road North during September 1978. *Author*

Above and right: On New Year's Day 1979 RMs 356, 479, 541 and 193, together with a pair of DMS Fleetlines, stand in the white stuff at Barking garage while, against the backdrop of Hainault Forest, Barking's RT1798 toils up Romford Road on route 62, the last RT-operated service. The 62 was due to be converted to RM operation on the same date as the 87, which meant that the RT class, entering service on 9 August 1939, would not have reached its 40th year of operation. However, staff refused to drive wider buses over Chadwell Heath station bridge, so the RTs carried on until 7 April 1979, the bridge problem being overcome by a re-routeing. *Author (both)*

Index of Locations

Abridge	Title page, 69
Aldenham	59
Apsley Mills	53
Barking	78
Barkingside	4
Bata Factory	66
Bishops Stortford	72
Bovingdon	5
Bushey Heath	58
Chigwell Row	17
Chingford	49
Corbets Tey	30
Cranham	40
East Purfleet	65
Elm Park	48
Epping	19, 24, 25, 26
Gidea Park	37
Grays	33, 34
Great Warley	67
Hainault	79
Harlow	12, 42
Hatfield	44, 45
Havering-atte-Bower	68
Hemel Hempstead	11, 13, 46, 61, 62
Hitchin	43, 54
Hornchurch	14
Ilford	32
Lambourne End	18
Loudwater Estate	36
Loughton	Back cover
Noak Hill	38, 39
Ockendon	34, 35
Potters Bar	60
Rainham	77
Rickmansworth	10
Romford	2, 7, 63, 73
St Albans	Front cover, 20, 21, 22, 27, 41, 52, 74
South Oxley	57
South Mimms	23
Stevenage	8, 31, 50, 51
Tring	15, 16
Upminster	28, 29
Waltham Cross	6
Wanstead	47
Ware	70, 71
Watford	9, 55, 75
Welham Green	76
Welwyn Garden City	56
West Tilbury	64